100
ACTION
SONGS!
FOR TODDLERS

We've selected rhymes and actions appropriate for toddlers. A few simple, familiar tunes have been used over and over so that two and three year olds can easily grasp the meaning of the words.

—The editors

100 ACTION SONGS FOR TODDLERS

Published by David C, Cook Publishing Co.
850 N. Grove Ave., Elgin, IL 60120
Cable address: DCCOOK

Designed by Christopher Patchel and Dawn Lauck

Printed in the United States of America.

ISBN 1-555513-146-8

Contents

Songs about Jesus and God

1 Help toddlers praise God by singing these words to the tune, *Row, Row, Row, Your Boat.*

Worship God today,
Worship with a clap.
   Clap hands on the word *clap*
Joyfully, joyfully, joyfully, joyfully,
   Clap hands in rhythm
Worship with a clap.
   Clap hands on the word *clap*

2 This rhyme, to the tune *Farmer in the Dell,* will help toddlers learn about God's creation.

First a flower is small;
   Crouch low
Then it grows so tall.
   Stand tall and stretch arms up
I like flowers big and small.
   Stand tall, then crouch low
I'm glad God made them all.
   Stand and clap hands

3 Let children pretend to swim or fly as you sing the following song to the tune of *Row, Row, Row Your Boat.*

Splish, splash, splish and splash.
Fish go swimming by.
God made fish both big and small,
They swim all day and night.

Flip, flap, flip and flap.
Birds go flying by.
God made birds both big and small,
They fly high in the sky.

4 Sing these words to the tune, *Old MacDonald Had a Farm,* as children hold hands and walk in a circle changing directions on each verse.

God made horses, sheep, and cows.
Neigh, neigh, baa, baa, moo.
The farmer cares for each of them.
God shows him what to do.

Farmers feed the animals hay.
Yum, yum, that tastes good.
God helps farmers grow the hay.
Because it is good food.

God made all the noisy squirrels.
Chatter, chee-chee, chee.
God made acorns, leaves, and nuts
For the squirrels to eat.

5 Sing this "story" about Zacchaeus to the tune of *Are You Sleeping?*

Where's Zacchaeus, where's Zacchaeus?
  Look around
In a tree, in a tree,
  Point up
Waiting to see Jesus, waiting to see Jesus.
  Shield eyes with hand
In a tree, in a tree.
  Point up

Here comes Jesus, here comes Jesus.
  Have fingers of right hand "walk" on left arm
Down the road, down the road.
Jesus sees Zacchaeus, Jesus sees Zacchaeus.
  Shield eyes with hand
In a tree, in a tree.
  Point up

Jesus told him, Jesus told him
To come down, to come down.
  Motion to come
Jesus helped Zacchaeus, Jesus helped Zacchaeus
Do what's right, do what's right.
  Clap hands

6 Sing these words to the tune of *The Farmer in the Dell.*

God loves us—it's true.
  Point to self
God loves us—it's true.
We can thank God for His love.
  Spread arms wide
God loves us—it's true.
  Point to self

Noah built an ark.
  Pretend to use hammer or saw
Noah built an ark.
Noah did what God told him.
  Cup hand behind ear.
Noah built an ark.
  Pretend to use hammer or saw

Moses crossed the Sea.
  March in place
Moses crossed the Sea.
Moses knew that God would help.
  Spread arms wide
Moses crossed the sea.
  March in place

Elijah got some food.
  Pretend to eat
Elijah got some food.
Elijah thanked God for His love.
  Pretend to pray
Elijah got some food.
  Pretend to eat

7 Teach this to the tune of *Mary Had a Little Lamb*. Have toddlers clap their hands every time they say the word, "Clap."

Show you love God with a clap,
With a clap, with a clap.
Show you love God with a clap,
Clap and clap and clap!

8 Sing this action rhyme to the tune of *Are You Sleeping?*

Who is Jesus? Who is Jesus?
　Shrug shoulders
He's God's Son? He's God's Son?
　Point up
Jesus is my Savior! Jesus is my Savior!
　Clap hands
He loves me! I love Him!
　Hug self

9 This song, to *The Farmer in the Dell*, will help toddlers learn to worship God.

I love God every day.
  Hug self
I love God every day.
  Hug self
I tell Him so each time I pray.
  Fold hands
I love God every day.
  Hug self

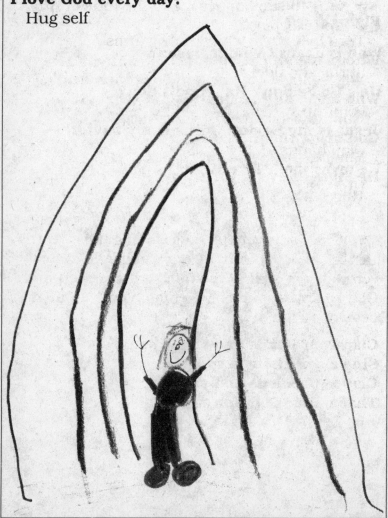

10 Help toddlers praise and worship God by singing these words to the tune of *Are You Sleeping?*

Who made mountains?
  Touch fingertips to make mountain
Who made sunshine?
  Touch fingertips overhead
Who made birds
  Wave arms
Flying free?
  Turn in a circle while waving arms
Who made all the spiders?
  Wiggle fingers of one hand on other arm
Who made all the flowers?
  Cup hands with wrists together
God made them.
  Spread arms wide
He loves me.
  Hug self

11 Clap in rhythm as you sing these words to *Mary Had a Little Lamb*. Add more verses by replacing "morning" with other things God has made such as evening, water, animals, people, and friends.

Clap your hands and sing a song,
Sing a song, sing a song.
Clap your hands and sing a song:
Thank You, God, for morning!

12 Use these words and actions to the tune of *London Bridge Is Falling Down*.

Who made the sun to light the day?
  Touch fingertips overhead
God did! God did!
God made the sun to light the day.
  Touch fingertips overhead
Thank You, God.

Who made stars that shine all night?
  Wiggle fingers in the air
God did! God did!
God made stars that shine all night.
  Wiggle fingers in the air
Thank You, God.

Who made fish and birds that fly?
  Put palms together and swish; flap arms
God did! God did!
God made fish and birds that fly.
  Put palms together and swish; flap arms
Thank You, God.

Who made grass and trees so tall?
  Wave arms in air
God did! God did!
God made grass and trees so tall.
  Wave arms in air
Thank You, God.

Who made dogs to run and play?
  Tap hands on knees
God did! God did!
God made dogs to run and play.
  Tap hands on knees
Thank You, God.

13 Have children clap as they thank God by singing this song to *Old MacDonald Had a Farm.*

God can hear me when I sing.
Joyfully, I say,
"Thank You, thank You, thank You, God,
For Your love today."

14 Teach toddlers about Jesus' love by singing these words to *London Bridge Is Falling Down.*

Jesus loves me very much,
   Hug self
Very much, very much.
Jesus loves me very much,
   Hug self
He's my friend.
   Clap hands

15

Talk to toddlers explaining that God hears us pray to Him no matter what we are doing. Then sing these words to the tune, *The Farmer in the Dell*.

When I hurt my knee
Rub knee
I can talk to God.
Fold hands to pray
God listens when I pray to Him;
Cup hand to ear
I can talk to God.
Fold hands to pray

Additional verses (add your own actions):
- **When I'm sick in bed**
- **When I'm feeling sad**
- **When I go to church**
- **When I go to sleep**
- **When I'm getting dressed**
- **When I'm eating lunch**
- **When I'm working hard**
- **When I lose my shoes**
- **When I help my dad**
- **When I'm having fun**
- **When I take a bath**

16 Sing these words to the tune of *Jesus Loves Me*. Have children clap or use rhythm instruments as they sing.

Little children sang for Him,
Sang for Jesus long ago.
I will sing a song for Him,
For I know He loves me so.

I know He loves me,
And I love Him, too.
Jesus, hear me sing,
My songs of praise to You!

17 Help toddlers learn about God by singing this to *Farmer in the Dell*.

God, You're very great!
Spread arms wide
You made the little bee!
Wiggle fingers by ear
You made the sun to shine for us.
Touch fingers overhead
I'm glad that You made me!
Point to self

18

Teach toddlers to thank God as they sing this to the tune *Jesus Loves Me*.

Thank You, God, for everything.
  Stretch arms wide
You're so very good to me!
  Point to self
Thank You, God, for all You do;
  Sweep arm to the right
Really, really I love You!
  Hug self; then point up

Yes, God, I love You.
Yes, God, I love You.
Yes, God, I love You.
I really do love You.

19 Teach this song about what Jesus taught to the tune, *Row, Row, Row Your Boat.*

Jesus teaches us
  Point up then to self
About God's love and care.
I can clap my hands and know
  Clap hands
That God is always there.

Jesus teaches us
  Point up, then to self
About God's love and care.
I can reach up high and know
  Stretch up high
That God is always there.

Jesus teaches us
  Point up, then to self
About God's love and care.
I can fold my hands and know
  Fold hands as if to pray
That God is always there.

Jesus teaches us
  Point up, then to self
About God's love and care.
I can give a hug and know
  Hug self
That God is always there.

20 Have children walk in a circle and clap as you sing these words to the tune *Farmer in the Dell.*

**I'm glad God gives to me
A home where I can play.
I'll thank Him for my family,
That cares for me each day.**

**I'm glad God gives to me
Good food to eat each day.
I'll thank Him for the gifts He gives
Each time I start to pray.**

21 Have toddlers clap in rhythm as they sing these words to *Mary Had a Little Lamb.*

**Talk to God at night and say,
"Thank You for a happy day."
When you wake in morning light,
Thank Him for a restful night.**

22 These words can be sung to the tune of *Mulberry Bush.*

Jesus always did good things,
　March in place
Did good things, did good things.
Jesus always did good things,
He taught His friends to pray.
　Fold hands

Jesus made sick people well,
　Reach up and stretch
People well, people well.
Jesus made sick people well,
And helped them to obey.
　Hold hands out, palms up

Here are other verses you could use:
- **Jesus helped the blind man see.**
- **Jesus helped the lame man walk.**

23 This action song to *Mary Had a Little Lamb*, teaches children things they can do for God.

I love You! Yes, I love You!
  Hug self, then point up
That is why I like to pray.
  Fold hands; bow head
I love You! Yes, I love You!
I pray to God each day!

I praise You! Yes, I praise You!
  Clap throughout this verse
That is why I like to sing.
I praise You! Yes, I praise You!
My praise to God I bring.

I thank You! Yes, I thank You!
  Nod head
That is why I like to give.
  Pretend to give an offering
I thank You! Yes, I thank You!
Everyday I live!

Songs about You and Me

24 Talk about all the things God cares for after you sing this to the tune *Skip to My Lou*.

Flowers grow in the rain and sun,
   Squat down; then slowly stand
Birds build nests in the trees, they do.
   Flap arms like a bird
God takes care of all of these.
   Clap hands
He takes care of me, too.
   Point to self.

God made animals, big and small,
   Spread arms wide; then bring together
Fish that swim in the sea—it's true!
   Make swimming motion
God takes care of all of these.
He takes care of me, too.
   Point to self.

25 Have children walk in a circle while singing these words to the tune of *London Bridge Is Falling Down*.

Jesus cares about His friends,
Young and old, big and small.
You are one of Jesus' friends!
Jesus loves you.

26 Sing these words to the tune, *Mulberry Bush*. Have toddlers use rhythm instruments as they they sing.

Jesus is a friend of mine,
He is with me all the time.
Inside, outside, near, or far,
He is near wherever we are.

27 Sing these words to *Happy Birthday* as children walk in a circle.

God gives us good rules,
That He'll help us obey.
Then we can be happy
At work and at play.

28 Sing these words and motions to the tune, *London Bridge Is Falling Down*.

God is with me when I jump,
  Jump on the word *jump*
When I jump, when I jump.
God is with me when I jump,
God is good!
  Clap hands

Here are other verses you can use, or think of your own:
• **God is with me when I sleep.**
  Rest head on folded hands
• **God is with me when I eat.**
  Pretend to eat

29

Sing this action rhyme is to the tune of *Mulberry Bush*.

I have clothes that I can zip,
   Pretend to zip jacket
I can zip, I can zip.
I am warm as I can be
God cares for me.
   Point to self.

I like ice cream I can lick,
   Pretend to lick ice cream cone
I can lick, I can lick
Two big scoops—oh boy, yippee!
God cares for me.
   Point to self.

God gave me a family,
   Clap hands
Family, family.
I'm glad He did that for you see
God cares for me.
   Point to self.

30 Sing this action rhyme to *Twinkle, Twinkle Little Star.*

God made Adam; God made Eve.
He made the first family.
God made you; God made me!
  Point to group, point to self
God made everyone we see.
God made every part of me,
  Point to self
My ears to hear; my eyes to see.
  Point to ears; point to eyes

31 Teach children this song to the tune of *Happy Birthday.*

I know Jesus loves you.
  Point to friend
I know Jesus loves me.
  Point to self
We all love one another
  Hug self
In God's family.
  Join hands to form circle

32 Have children clap their hands as they sing these words to *Farmer in the Dell.*

I'm Jesus' special friend.
I'm Jesus' special friend.
He helps me know what's right to do.
I'm Jesus' special friend!

33 Sing this rhyme to *Mulberry Bush* as toddlers hold hands and walk in a circle.

You and I will be kind today,
Kind today, kind today.
You and I will be kind today,
To everyone we see.

Here are other verses you might use:
• **You and I will say, "Hi" today.**
• **You and I will smile today.**

34 Use this action rhyme to teach toddlers that Jesus cares about them no matter how they feel. Sing it to *Mary Had a Little Lamb*.

Jesus cares if you are sad,
    Make a sad face
If you're big or if you're small.
    Stretch tall, then squat
Jesus wants you to be happy.
    Clap hands
He cares about us all.
    Spread arms wide

35 This action rhyme about prayer is also sung to *Farmer in the Dell.*

I can talk to God,
  Point to self, then up
I can talk to God,
  Point to self, then up
God listens when I pray to Him,
  Point up, then fold hands in prayer
I can talk to God.
  Point to self, then up

36 Toddlers will enjoy clapping to this happy song as they sing it to the tune of *Did You Ever See a Lassie?*

I'm so glad we have the Bible,
The Bible, the Bible.
I'm so glad we have the Bible
To learn of our friend.
Our friend's name is Jesus.
Our friend's name is Jesus.
I'm so glad we have the Bible
To learn of our friend.

37 This fun song, to the tune of *Ten Little Indians,* teaches about the love of Jesus.

Listen! Listen! Jesus loves me.
  Point to ears; then to self
Listen! Listen! Jesus loves you.
  Point to ears; then to others
Let's go out and tell our friends
  Cup hands around mouth
That Jesus loves us all!
  Hug self

38 Sing these words to the tune, *Good Night, Ladies.* Have children point to the part of the body the song talks about (you can add other verses for knees, ears, feet, and so on), or have children do the actions the words tell them.

Where is your nose?
Where is your nose?
Where is your nose?
Thank God for your nose.

Sit right down now.
Sit right down now.
Fold your hands now.
Thank God for everything.

39 Sing this action rhyme to the tune, *Mary Had a Little Lamb*. Then talk to the children about how God cares for all that He has created.

I'm a flower growing tall,
  Stoop down and rise slowly
Growing tall, growing tall.
I'm a flower growing tall.
God takes care of me.
  Clap hands

God will send the sunshine bright,
  Touch fingertips overhead
Sunshine bright, sunshine bright.
God will send the sunshine bright.
God takes care of me.
  Clap hands

I'm a bird that flies so high,
  Flap arms up and down
Flies so high, flies so high.
I'm a bird that flies so high.
God takes care of me.
  Clap hands

God gives twigs to build a nest,
  Cup hands to form a nest
Build a nest, build a nest.
God gives twigs to build a nest.
God takes care of me.
  Clap hands

40 Here's another rhyme about God's care for us. Sing it to the tune, *Farmer in the Dell.*

God gives the birds their food.
   Flap arms up and down
God gives the birds their food.
But God loves me much more than these.
He takes good care of me!

God makes the flowers grow.
   Stoop down and rise slowly
God makes the flowers grow.
But God loves me much more than these.
He takes good care of me!

41 Let toddlers hold hands and walk in a circle as they sing these words to the tune, *Farmer in the Dell.*

God gives us food to eat,
God gives us food to eat.
He gives us farmers who can help.
God gives us food to eat.

God knows our every need,
God knows our every need.
He gives us people who can help.
God knows our every need.

42 Sing this action song to *London Bridge Is Falling Down.*

God said we should work six days,
  Pretend to hammer
Work six days, work six days.
He gives us rules to obey
Because He loves us.
  Hug self

God said we should go to church,
  Walk in place
Go to church, go to church.
He gives us rules to obey
Because He loves us.
  Hug self

God said we should love each other,
  Put an arm around a friend
Love each other, love each other.
He gives us rules to obey
Because He loves us.
  Hug self

43
Have children sing this action rhyme to the tune, *Row, Row, Row Your Boat.*

I'm glad God made plants,
Pretty, pretty plants.
I'm glad God made the tall oak tree.
  Stretch arms high
And that God made me.
  Point up, then to self

I'm glad God made spring,
Pretty, pretty spring.
I'm glad God made the rain we see,
  Wiggle fingers like falling rain
And that God made me.
  Point up, then to self

I'm glad God made birds,
Pretty, pretty birds.
  Flap arms like wings
I'm glad God made the bumblebee,
  Wiggle fingers near your face
And that God made me.
  Point up, then to self

44

This rhyme teaches toddlers to give thanks. Sing it to the tune, *London Bridge Is Falling Down*.

I thank God for trees and flowers,
Fold hands as if in prayer.
Trees and flowers, trees and flowers.
I thank God for trees and flowers,
I know they come from You.
Clap hands

Other verses:

• **I thank God for day and night.**
Point up to the sun; rest cheek on hands
• **I thank God for food I eat.**
Pretend to eat.

45

Sing this fun song to the tune, *Twinkle, Twinkle Little Star*. Have children do what the words say.

Touch your knees
And touch your nose.
Touch your head
Then your toes.
Touch your stomach,
Touch your eye.
Bend down low
Then reach up high.
Turn around,
And look and see
God made everyone
Wonderfully.

46 Sing these words to the tune, *Mary Had a Little Lamb*. Have children walk around the room with a friend while singing this rhyme.

Who loves me when I am good?
God does! God does!
When I do the things I should,
Yes, God loves me!

Who loves me when I feel bad?
God does! God does!
Even though He, too, feels sad,
Yes, God loves me!

Every day, who cares for me?
God does! God does!
When I'm sad, as sad can be,
God cares for me!

47 Sing this action rhyme to the tune, *Twinkle, Twinkle Little Star*.

Here're my hands to work for God.
  Hold out hands
Here're my ears and here're my eyes.
  Point to ears, then eyes
I want to watch and listen, too,
  Shape hands like binoculars, then cup them
  behind ears
For the jobs that're just my size.
Here're my hands to work for God.
  Hold out hands
Here're my ears and here're my eyes.
  Point to ears, then eyes

48 Teach toddlers how specially God made them by singing these words to *Farmer in the Dell.*

God gave me legs to stand,
 Stand up
And arms so I can stretch.
 Stretch
God made me very specially.
 Point up, then to self
God made me.
 Point up, then to self

God gave me feet to run,
 Run in place
And hands so I can clap.
 Clap
God made me very specially.
 Point up, then to self
God made me.
 Point up, then to self

God gave me a head to nod,
 Nod
And eyes so I can blink.
 Shut, open eyes
God made me very specially.
 Point up, then to self
God made me.
 Point up, then to self

49 This little rhyme, to the tune *Mulberry Bush*, teaches children about praying.

When I pray, I talk to God,
Fold hands in prayer
Talk to God, talk to God.
God hears everything I say
Cup hand behind ear
When I talk to Him.
Fold hands in prayer

50 Sing this short little rhyme to the tune, *Twinkle, Twinkle Little Star.*

God cares for me
While I'm small,
Bend low
Just as He will
When I'm tall.
Stand tall

51 Teach toddlers this action rhyme to *Happy Birthday.*

My two ears can hear,
Point to ears
My two eyes can see.
Point to eyes
It's God who made us,
Raise arms
Both you and me.
Point to another, then to self

Songs about Family and Friends

52 Have children clap and walk in a circle as they sing these words to *The Farmer in the Dell.*

My parents help me grow.
My parents help me grow.
They give me love and food and clothes.
My parents help me grow.

My teacher helps me grow.
My teacher helps me grow.
She (He) helps me learn what I should
  know.
My teacher helps me grow.

God helps us all to grow.
God helps us all to grow.
He gives us everyone we need
To help us all to grow.

53 Sing this action rhyme to the tune, *Mary Had a Little Lamb.*

Baby elephant swings his trunk,
  Bend over, join hands for trunk
Like his father and his mother.
  Same action
God gave me a family, too,
  Point to self
And we love each other.
  Hug self

54 Have children walk in a circle as they sing this to *Mulberry Bush*. Sing more verses by using names of other family members.

We can thank God for our moms,
For our moms, for our moms.
We can thank God for our moms.
Thank You, God.

55 Have children do what this action song says as they sing it to the tune, *Are You Sleeping?*

Let's be friends.
Let's be friends.
Clap with me.
Clap with me.
Come and clap with me.
Come and clap with me.
Clap. Clap. Clap.
Clap. Clap. Clap.

In place of *clap* use other action words such as hop, march, smile, and hug.

56 Before you sing these words to the tune, *Farmer in the Dell*, talk with toddlers about ways they can show love to others. Do motions for their suggestions as you sing these words.

Now we can show our love.
Now we can show our love.
We show our love as Jesus did.
Now we can show our love.

57 Sing these words to *Mulberry Bush* as you lead children in these actions.

Won't you come and march with me,
March with me, march with me?
Won't you come and march with me?
I'm glad that I can march.

Other verses could include the actions clap, jump, run, sit, or pray.

58 Sing these words to the tune, *Row, Row, Row Your Boat.*

One friend and one friend,
   Hold up one finger on each hand
Together they do know
   Hold fingers together
That a friend always loves you,
   Hug self
For God has made them so!
   Stretch arms wide

59 Have children hold hands with a friend and walk in a circle as they sing this rhyme to the tune, *Farmer in the Dell.*

It's good to have a friend.
It's good to have a friend.
Together we have lots of fun.
It's good to have a friend.

Songs about Helping

60 Teach children about helping by singing these words to the tune, *Mary Had a Little Lamb.* Think of other ways that toddlers can help such as pick up toys or set the table. Use these for additional verses.

I can help to feed my pets,
    Pretend to set out bowl; pour food.
Feed my pets, feed my pets.
I can help to feed my pets;
I can help at home.
    Clap hands and smile.

Helping makes me happy, yes!
    Clap hands and smile.
Happy, yes; happy, yes!
Helping makes me happy, yes,
When I help at home!
    Clap and smile.

61 Have toddlers march around the room as they sing these words to the tune of *Farmer in the Dell.*

How can I be good?
How can I be good?
Jesus helps me every day.
He helps me to be good.

I can share my toys.
I can share my toys.
Jesus helps me every day.
He helps me to be good.

62 You can use this action rhyme to the tune, *Mulberry Bush* to help toddlers learn to dress themselves.

This is the way we put on our boots,
   Pretend to pull on boots
Put on our boots,
Put on our boots.
This is the way we put on our boots,
On a winter morning.

Here are some additional verses you can use for the other seasons.
- **This is the way we put up an umbrella**
   Pretend to put up an umbrella
On a rainy, spring day.
- **This is the way we wear a sun hat**
   Pretend to put on a hat
On a summer morning.
- **This is the way we put on a jacket**
   Pretend to put on a jacket
On a cool, fall morning.

63 Sing this fun action rhyme to the tune of *Mary Had a Little Lamb*.

Pat the cat and puppy dog.
   Stroke one hand on the back of the other
Pick up things for your Mother.
   Bend down and touch floor
Smile and wave "hello" to friends.
   Smile and wave
Be kind to one another.
   Spread arms wide

64 Toddlers will enjoy marching around the room with a friend as they sing these words to the tune, *Twinkle, Twinkle Little Star.*

**We want to be kind and good,
Just as Jesus says we should.
Loving others every day,
Helping them in some small way.
We want to be kind and good,
Just as Jesus says we should.**

65 Use this simple song to the tune of *Mulberry Bush* when you want the children to prepare for different activities. Vary the verses as you wish.

**Let's all put our toys away,
Toys away, toys away.
We will talk and listen to stories.
Let's put our toys away.**

**Let's all put our toys away,
Toys away, toys away.
We have listened and talked and played.
And now it's time to go.**

66 Use this action rhyme to tell toddlers when it's time to pick up toys or follow some other instruction. Sing this rhyme to the tune, *Twinkle, Twinkle Little Star.*

Hurry, scurry, 1, 2, 3.
  Clap as you sing the numbers
Listen, listen carefully.
Time to put toys back in place.
Then put on a happy face.
Listen, listen carefully,
  Pause with hand cupped behind ear
Hurry, scurry, 1, 2, 3!
  Clap as you sing the numbers

67 Sing these words to the tune, *Are You Sleeping?* Use them to teach children by adding a motion at the end of the song such as a helping activity or stretching exercise.

I am growing, I am growing,
Wise and tall, wise and tall.
See what I can do now.
See what I can do now.
Do it, too; do it, too.

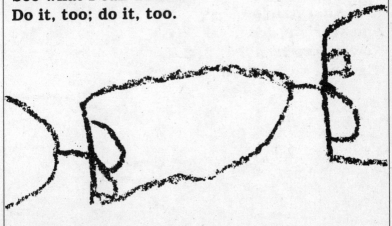

68 This rhyme is full of actions that will prepare children for a story, snack, or any listening time. Sing it slowly so toddlers can follow the motions to the tune, *Ten Little Indians*

Reach up high,
Then touch the ground.
Wave "hello,"
Then turn around.
Pat your head,
Then give a clap.
Sit right down with your
Hands in your lap.

69 Here's another rhyme that helps prepare children to listen. Sing it to *Twinkle, Twinkle Little Star*.

Reach way up.
Then touch your toes,
Hands on shoulders,
Hands on nose.
Clap three times,
And turn around.
Fold your hands
And sit right down.
Now you're ready, 1, 2, 3,
'Cause it's time to listen to me.

70 Here's the third rhyme you can use to get children's attention. Have them do what the words say as you sing the rhyme to the tune, *Are You Sleeping?*

Clap up high, clap up high.
Clap down low, clap down low.
Now clap in the middle, now clap in the
   middle.
And down you go! Down you go!
   Sit with hands folded

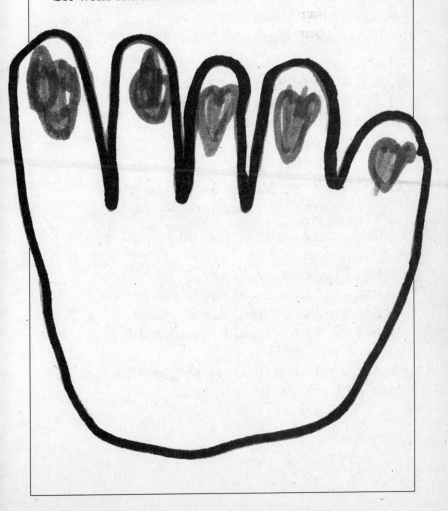

71 Use this song, to the tune of *Mulberry Bush*, to help toddlers get ready to listen to a story or special instructions.

Let's all play a listening game,
A listening game,
A listening game.
Let's all play a listening game,
Listen very closely.

72 Sing this fun rhyme that helps young children learn about God's creation to the tune, *Mary Had a Little Lamb*.

What kind of animal says, "Arf, arf"?
Says, "Arf, arf"? Says, "Arf, arf"?
What kind of animal says, "Arf, arf"?
Can you guess its name?

What kind of plant smells, oh, so nice?
Oh, so, nice? Oh, so, nice?
What kind of plant smells, oh, so nice?
Can you guess its name?

Here are some other ideas and actions for different animals:
- **What kind of animal says: "Moo, moo"?**
- **What kind of animal says: "Baa, baa"?**
- **What kind of animal says: "Oink, oink"?**
- **What kind of animal hops like this?**
  Hop like bunnies
- **What kind of animal walks like this?**
  Walk like dogs, ducks, and so forth

Songs about Church and Sunday School

73 This action rhyme, to the tune *Farmer in the Dell*, will teach children about worshiping together in church.

Together we will pray
   Fold hands in prayer
And sing joyfully.
   Clap hands two times
We're glad that we are here in church
   Point to selves
With all God's family.
   Spread arms wide

74 Have children march around the room as they sing these words to the tune, *Mary Had a Little Lamb*. Don't forget to have them tell you what's their favorite thing to do.

We like to come to Sunday school,
To learn and sing and to play.
What's *your* favorite thing to do
On this God's special day?

75 This song can be used to introduce the Bible story during Sunday school. Sing the words to the tune, *London Bridge Is Falling Down*. Use these words when telling the story of the miraculous catch of fish.

We are going to catch some fish,
Catch some fish,
Catch some fish.
We are going to catch some fish,
Catch some fish today.

Try to think of words that would be suitable for other stories as well such as:
• **God told Noah to build an ark.**
• **David was a shepherd boy.**

76
Sing these words about Sunday school to *Farmer in the Dell.*

At Sunday school, my friends
  Hold hands
And I learn how to pray.
  Fold hands, bow head
We're learning to love Jesus
  Hug self
And learning to obey.
  Clap hands

77
Have children sing these words to the tune of *Twinkle, Twinkle Little Star.*

Church is such a happy place.
  Clap hands
See my smiling, happy face.
  Smile
It is where I laugh and sing
  Skip in a circle
And where I bring my offering.
Church is such a happy place.
  Clap hands
See my smiling, happy face.
  Smile

78 Teach children that God is a special friend by singing these words to the familiar tune of *Jesus Loves Me*. Have them play rhythm instruments as they sing.

God's a special friend of mine.
He listens to me when I pray.
He wants us all to come to church
On this, His very special day.
Refrain:
God is my friend.
God is my friend.
God is my friend.
This is His special day.

79 This is another song that you can make up lots of different verses as you sing it to the tune of *Farmer in the Dell* or *Row, Row, Row*.

We can sing at church.
We can sing at church.
Come along and join our song.
We can sing at church.

Who can beat the drum?
Who can beat the drum?
Come along and join our song!
Who can beat the drum?

• We can worship God.
• Who can clap their hands?

80 *Mary Had a Little Lamb* is a good melody to use to sing this action rhyme. These words help teach young children what to do at church.

Let us sing our happiest songs,
   Point to mouth
Let us bring an off'ring to share.
   Extend cupped hands
Come and let us worship God
   Beckon to children
And thank Him with a prayer.
   Fold hands

81 Toddlers will enjoy this simple song to the tune of *London Bridge Is Falling Down.* Have them walk in a circle and clap their hands as they sing.

Oh, we love to go to church,
Go to church, go to church.
Oh, we love to go to church.
To worship God.

82 These words, sung to *Mulberry Bush*, teach children what to do in church.

This is the way we pray to God,
  Fold hands; bow head
Pray to God, pray to God.
This is the way we pray to God,
Each and every day.
- **This is the way we sing to God.**
  Pretend to look at a songbook
- **This is the way we give to God.**
  Pretend to give offering
- **This is the way we listen to stories.**
  Cup hands around ears

Songs about Christmas

83 Give toddlers bells to shake as they sing this Christmas rhyme to *Jingle Bells*.

Ring these bells.
Ring these bells.
Ring them loud and clear.
Jesus Christ is born today.
Let's ring the bells all year!

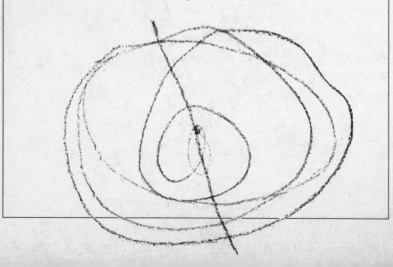

84 Sing this simple action song to the tune of *Mulberry Bush*.

My face can smile; my hands can clap.
  Point to smile; then clap two times
My face can smile; my hands can clap.
My face can smile; my hands can clap.
I'm happy 'cause it's Christmas!
  Spread arms wide

85 Sing these words slowly so toddlers can imitate the words and actions. Use the tune *Happy Birthday*.

A Savior's been born!
  Cup hands around mouth
Hurry up! We can run
  Run in place
To see baby Jesus.
  Circle eyes with fingers
God sent us His Son.
  Fold arms as if rocking baby

86 Have toddlers march around the room clapping as they sing these words to the tune of *Skip to My Lou*.

We can praise Him with a clap.
We can praise Him with a clap.
We can praise Him with a clap.
God sent His Son Jesus.

87 Even very young children will enjoy and understand this simple action song. Have them clap as they sing it to the tune, *Mulberry Bush.*

Sing a song and clap your hands.
Clap your hands, clap your hands.
Sing a song and clap your hands.
Happy birthday, Jesus!

88 Sing these words to the tune, *The Farmer in the Dell.* If you wish, children could act out the verses as if they were putting on a Christmas play. You could even provide simple costumes. Have them clap as they sing the first verse; repeat that verse at the end as well.

Oh, happy Christmastime.
Oh, happy Christmastime.
We're glad that baby Jesus came
At happy Christmastime!

The cows and sheep were there.
The cows and sheep were there.
We're glad that baby Jesus came
At happy Christmastime!

The shepherds hear the news.
The shepherds hear the news.
We're glad that baby Jesus came
At happy Christmastime!

The Wise Men saw the star.
The Wise Men saw the star.
We're glad that baby Jesus came
At happy Christmastime!

89 Sing this action rhyme to the tune of *Happy Birthday*.

Baby Jesus came to earth,
And He was very small.
  Pretend to hold baby
God sent us little Jesus
Because He loves us all!
  Point up, then hug self

90 This action song can be sung to *Twinkle, Twinkle, Little Star*.

Baby Jesus sleeping in the hay;
  Rest your head on your hands
Shepherds kneeling as they pray,
  Kneel; fold hands in prayer
Thanking God for sending His Son
  Point up
Thanking Him for all He's done.
Baby Jesus sleeping in the hay;
  Rest your head on your hands
On this special Christmas Day.
  Clap hands

91 Have children sing this song to the tune, *Mulberry Bush.*

Mary rocks her baby boy,
   Pretend to rock baby
Baby boy, baby boy.
Then she lays Him down to sleep
   Pretend to put baby and go sh-h-h
In a manger bed.

Animals and shepherds watch
   Shield eyes with hands
Little baby Jesus.
Lying there so quietly
   Pretend to sleep; rest head on hands
On His bed of hay.

92 To the tune of *Ten Little Indians,* sing the first verse softly, putting a finger to your lips when you say, "Sh." Sing the second verse loudly, clapping when you say, "Thanks."

Sh! Sh!
See the baby Jesus.
Sh! Sh!
Sleeping on the hay.
Sh! Sh!
See the baby Jesus.
Born on Christmas Day.

Thanks! Thanks!
Thank You, God, for Jesus.
Thanks! Thanks!
Thank You for Your Son.
Thanks! Thanks!
Thank You, God, for Jesus.
Joy for everyone.

93 Have children walk in a circle as they sing these words to *London Bridge Is Falling Down.*

God loved us and sent His Son,
Sent His Son, sent His Son.
God loved us and sent His Son,
His Son Jesus.

94 Here's another simple Christmas action song that young children will enjoy. Sing it to the tune of *Skip to My Lou.*

Hear the news the angels sing.
   Point to ears
Hear the news the angels sing.
Hear the news the angels sing.
God sent His Son, Jesus.
   Clap hands

Shepherds run to Bethlehem.
   Run in place
Shepherds run to Bethlehem.
Shepherds run to Bethlehem.
God sent His Son, Jesus.
   Clap hands

We can praise Him with a clap.
   Clap hands throughout verse
We can praise Him with a clap.
We can praise Him with a clap.
God sent His Son, Jesus.

Songs about Easter

95 Let toddlers march around the room as they sing this happy song to the tune, *London Bridge Is Falling Down.*

**Easter is a special time
So let's sing a happy song.
Alleluia! Allelu!
You can sing along.**

96 Sing these words to the tune of *Are You Sleeping?*

Girls and boys, sing for joy.
  Cup hands around mouth
Easter day! Celebrate!
  Stretch out arms
Jesus is alive, Jesus is alive!
  Clap hands
Sing for joy, sing for joy.
  Cup hands around mouth

97 Sing this action rhyme slowly so young children will be able to follow the words and motions. Use the tune, *Ten Little Indians*.

Clap your hands!
Clap twice
The sun is shining.
Touch fingertips overhead
Clap your hands
Clap twice
And shout "Hooray!"
Cup hands around mouth
Clap your hands,
Clap twice
For Jesus loves us.
Hug self
He's *alive* today!
Squat down; then jump up on "alive"

98 This action rhyme can be sung to the tune of *Mary Had a Little Lamb*.

Morning sun is shining bright.
Touch fingertips overhead
Wear a smile this happy day!
Point to smile
Clap your hands now, 1, 2, 3.
Clap as you sing the numbers
Jesus is alive—hooray!
Jump on the word "hooray"

99 This song, to the tune of *Happy Birthday*, provides a good opportunity for toddlers to use rhythm instruments. Sing it through a couple of times before they "play" their instruments.

I'm so glad for Easter.
It's such a special day!
Jesus came back to life,
He's alive today!

I'm so glad for Easter.
It's such a special day!
Let's tell the Good News—
Jesus still lives today!

100 After singing these words to the tune of *Mary Had a Little Lamb*, teach children that they talk to Jesus when they pray.

Jesus is my special friend,
  Skip in a circle
Special friend, special friend.
Jesus is my special friend,
And He's alive today.
  Clap hands

Jesus listens when I pray,
  Cup hand behind ear; then fold hands
When I pray, when I pray.
Jesus listens when I pray,
For He's alive today.
  Clap hands